THIS WAS THE RIVER

JOHN PASS

This Was the River

HARBOUR
PUBLISHING

HARBOUR PUBLISHING CO. LTD.
P.O. Box 219, Madeira Park, BC, VON 2H0
www.harbourpublishing.com

Cover image: Detail from "Creation of the Animals" by Tintoretto, oil on canvas c. 1551
Edited by Silas White
Cover design by Anna Comfort O'Keeffe
Text design by Shed Simas / Onça Design
Printed and bound in Canada
Printed on 100% recycled paper

Harbour Publishing acknowledges the support of the Canada Council for the Arts, which last year invested $153 million to bring the arts to Canadians throughout the country.

Nous remercions le Conseil des arts du Canada de son soutien. L'an dernier, le Conseil a investi 153 millions de dollars pour mettre de l'art dans la vie des Canadiennes et des Canadiens de tout le pays.

We also gratefully acknowledge financial support from the Government of Canada and from the Province of British Columbia through the BC Arts Council and the Book Publishing Tax Credit.

Library and Archives Canada Cataloguing in Publication

Title: This was the river / John Pass.
Names: Pass, John, 1947- author.
Description: Poems.
Identifiers: Canadiana (print) 20190148772 | Canadiana (ebook) 20190148802 |
     ISBN 9781550178753 (softcover) | ISBN 9781550178760 (HTML)
Classification: LCC PS8581.A77 T55 2019 | DDC C811/.54—dc23

for Theresa—

currents, eddies &
aspen, beech, cotoneaster, pine

Contents

A Cheering Stain

Creation of the Animals

This Was the River

A CHEERING STAIN

The Weight Against Beginning

How honour here the weight against beginning
shouldered a year or more believing
it familiar and negotiable, seeking fulcrum

over this phrase or that journey, purchase
in the old approaches, grip for the tip slipping
against what's done and done, correctly

stolid, not to be shifted? Limbless
heaviness so many slop and wallow in: sour,
opinionated. Or busy in some worthy, tiresome way

about the world, themselves. How intractable
it is, the life one wanted, even unto
its deliverance accomplished into time

not needed now to create it. It's created. Needs
but living out. Needs. And these tools unwieldy.

Rereading My Notes re Rereading *Clea* in Venice

Clearer, or me more at ease over years intervening
with ambiguity? Magnificence and monument emerge
and merge in mist, marginally greyer in the whitish grey

daylight where canals curve or sway towards them. I get
the puns now I say, the literary ones, but make no
specific reference. I have Pursewarden's sense

of art as heraldic tableau of events specific
to the life of each artist become fluent, universal.
Moody, watery, Mediterranean mind. Mine inviting its gilt

and oils towards shimmer in darks a world away: flats
between leaf mulch and earth, the under-shadow
of salal edging rock bluff. So I might go
not murkily under arches, domes, into

niches, alcoves human in their curvature, stations of presence
and departure in places as foreign to forest as parts
of the old brain become to each other, causeways

and narrow cobble overgrown,
acculturated. So I might go newly
native in the soft wash and moss of the quiet city.

Open Question

Density and depth of green pushed into
and insular where the house is. Promise
fulfilled. Appalled I can't build further

upon that. A little light sifting up
from the lake in the morning. Or rain
an aggrieved grey in the foreground. Under-

storey gaping, ever-tendered unyielding
invitation, never located as the lucky
find of pine mushrooms

by footfall or a flicker (the bird)
in the treetops. *Forest bathing*
a new age recommends, surrender

of focus in a middle distance to misty
whatever. And even Wendell Berry, devoted
old seer on a log sitting, defaults a posteriori

to the earth, "as ever, itself. Free.
A bargain! Get it while it lasts." Spirit restored,
Christian or pagan, too soon a departure. Too soon

come home to the self-same endangered stasis, or
the trees just trees. Clearing, a cul-de-sac, full

stops to pull on the open question.

A Cheering Stain

I wake up every day wanting
to do, walk out every day under

fundamentals, trees
moreso than buildings, a heavy air

moreso than either, breathing no answer.

Why complicate the old confusions?
We've always been fogged and must

condense, mould. Icy hose disconnected
contents, you I wait out, curlicue, clueless.

You I hold self-evident, drop, don't
bring indoors. Branch and saw. Twists

thaw and seep and surge towards
finality? In house we lumber, delay

and ingenuity. What wants doing?

≈

Over the berm of the observed if I
could venture in a trusted tongue
you'd want me to speak (I must)

to the terrible extrapolations—a globe
warming... Is that the glow mistaken

for sunrise? Otherwise dark wall
of forest, mossy grave-mound

in the foreground of a cat
come back, but farther went its sister

so far my grown-up daughter teases
me ten years after, *What would you do*

if Cloudy sauntered today
into our clearing? I'd say

Cloudy will always be with us,
or some such facile nonsense

as the statistical engines grapple
with how high the oceans might rise

to the numberless human occasions
anticipated in 2100. How much of this

rainforest timber shroud will be tinder
or ash by then? You too, reader, lost there in

this, in them? So quickly we're losing
momentum going forward not

homeward crumb to crumb and the years
as ever just begun, and the day...

≈

Impossibly into the emptiness north-
wards, light. And thinking, taking sides, slides

like Frost's ice on a stove or the headlong stride
of the grouse from cover of salal to cover

of salal, its lovely complex multi-striated browns
and greys and blacks a life's work if wanted

in lieu of the fitful, cheering stain

of pink in the sky near that opening, atmosphere's
blowhole, a whole planet breaching. Each

thought, grouse, life's work—like
the ice the master taught went poem's way (its
own, individual) didn't. Everything's gravity

takes over this edge or that, and pools anew.

≈

Motionless alders in mist/drizzle/drip, one last
brown leaf in an awkward attachment above
mush of leaf litter underfoot.

Murk-green backdrop, whitish dull sky behind cedars, whitish lake.
Flat-line landscape, steady state, lateral before lift: little swing/dip
upward dogwood twigs take at each leaf node intersection. Yes

I'm sweet on the dipper's knee-
bend and bounce, on its blink and beak tilt—
sweet on the sprightly yerba buena and ochre
witches' butter, sweet

on spring, on the deepening pond
but this is colourlessly closer

to the damage we've done, to something as close
we can never damage, longer
(naturally) than life.

Through the Ice

...but warm enough somehow
to tread water in shabby workboots, boost

out. Only loss the camera I had
in hand, folded wet wallet intact.

All my knee-high splashing gasped awk-
wardness grasping (through interweave

of trees above) a dreamy smudge. Daylight.

Simply Really Looking

Tim Daw, groundskeeper at Stonehenge,
having noticed in this year's exceptionally

dry summer parched areas of grass
where in the ancient structure stones

(now missing) must have been, says:

I am still amazed
and very pleased

that simply really looking at something,
that tens of thousands of people had

unwittingly seen, can reveal secrets
that sophisticated machinery can't.

New Town Hall

Kitty-corner across Charles Square
from Pizzeria Donna new meaning

is but the façade of a moment
where rivulets curl in relief past

and under blank shields in floral
cedillas or inverted question marks

between the windows. Puzzlement
itself is satisfaction. Its not-knowing

traction displaces the displacement
of being new anywhere, having placemat

and ballpoint (no bald point)
to hand, and something to read.

CREATION OF THE ANIMALS

...when
staring into light
we think
— Frank O'Hara

Creation of the Animals

after Tintoretto

Eleven frantic one-eyed fishes fleeing
the appliqué God! He is all cloak and beatific full-
body nimbus aloft at the sea's edge in a streaky dawn

(in air as yet half-made, unawakened) and they
are all surging upward, half out of their element in
terror. A turtle in the murk. Land animals stricken

or galloping in His wake: dazed elk, startled doe's head.
A splotchy dog snuffles the beach beside rabbits. Flocks athwart
the sky: geese-like, pheasant-like, ibis-like. Each likeness paired, a-wing

in unison. Thirty-five, maybe, species in all.
Everything headlong and muddled, chary

compelled in a like direction as if before fire
compelled in a fraught dimension as if after.

Squirrel

Okay you frantics, squabblers, fur-fist bodies
thrown at each other across the seed-husk barrens
beneath the bird feeder, chunterers—

you can have January. Noisy in my stead, noise
in my head, you've stood my ground, held the fort—
those condos you've made of my firewood stacked
in the shed—me crozzling, despairing in my cave

of health scare, TV after too much dinner, numb
and silent. Hysterics make fair sense and complement
then, okay. But the light now arriving for breakfast

is nuanced in westerly indigos so latish I sip
my wine and nibble my olive in it. Time

to get human again (routinely
reactionary) and rake up
our mess, rebuild

the garden over the drain field. Don't misunderstand.
I'll not deny thanks for your rude, hyperthyroid
sustaining, your beady ogle. I've seen you

rooting in creases of branch along the beam. I know the seeds
of the dream I love to live in (the day upon day of worthy
work and better sleeping) are hard-won and hidden

in aberrant being, abhorrent behaviour. Chitter on. Ascend
the sunlit, windy trees. Near enough to kick you gluttonous
under ferns, I'm raggedly appending here, speaking up

for feathery balancing fronds of tail, end-frailties
we fly with given half a sky and our whole nature.

Elk

Dusk through the window but mocha glow enough
from his fine hide to catch an eye. Seep

of dusk from forest dark into the smudgy
softnesses, soft ground nigh the garden his hooves

imprint deeply (we see later). Sleep I pull
you from to glimpse him sort of, young bull

no flash of photo nor insight can push to entirely.
His herd we hear breaking about in the bush.

Big fern by the bench munched (we see later)
and the mid-height, mid-size boughs of ornamental

cherry mangled and stripped. The way back across
the highway and up the hydro line. Dusk in the circuits

where the draft lies. Dusk on the screen. New leaf
a paler, brighter green. We see later. Up the mountain

and here too, here now, everywhere (listen!)
the sun's one syllable bellowing morning.

Deer

Waiting for anything new about deer.
Waiting for everything known about deer.
Waiting for a path to open through the underbrush

stranded here species of watchful waiting, soft-
bodied, straddling salal inside

invisibly pixellated environs (densely specific loci
of alertness) who might stride gingerly off or

leap into your swerve. Sinew and twitch and stilted
stepping is our signature through browse, through ponder,

through what's left of your garden, your uneventful
drive home. Who would carry work gloves

to drag the famous corpse/trope to the shoulder
of yet another North American poem, or returning
in them and an old jacket find only smears

of snot and blood on the asphalt? Who'd get lucky
in the interim, tossing the venison into their pulled-over
pickup? Not us. First time walking the land we'd asked
the realtor (of all people) re the pressed moss hollows

below the bluff: (she) *Do deer sleep here?* And,
(me) *would these be good places*
for the well?

It's aquifer not ground-
water, drilled to through granite you want
with the head near the house... The springy

(still hanging) first question's still dreaming
still pressing dimensions of presence, succulent
destinations: sapling in the pre-dawn, patio shade

under climber roses, caged peas. Statuesque, testing
the breeze up the driveway, or in the orchard a

low-limbed leaf cluster in a forelimbed
up-pawing hoof-scrabble and   stretch, it listens.

Coyote

The bright ungainly landscapes/sound-
scapes scraping, tectonic: pack hardly shifting

off centre-line roadkill in a lone car's light
tunnel; wintry grunts and squeals unmistakably sex

slid down hill under us waking. Wake up! Think
there's a slinking by, or word-craft to leg-trap

the drift? Wily's not the half of it. The body
itself glimpsed flickering in golden grass

on the traffic island, gone, keeps going.
Or an ambulance siren prompts in passing

yelp and moan from the deep bush, den
that close to home and then the pup

emerges August mornings in haphazard
walkabout through the yard. Across the sun-

splotchy pastoral he's pausing, performing
that most disarming of canine gestures: soft-

mouthed drag and tug (through milk teeth and
new incisors) of berries from the pawed-down

shrub. Omnivorous
as us. As us-hungry maybe?
Hungry for *usness*, with us? The us

mussed together in talkabout blather
and gather at the stair top to see

him enter the disused doghouse, turn and
peruse for one heartbeat the ground-shifty

view? The us deep-dishing, wide-angling the instant
he's through that, that jaws and yaws away on one?

Dragonfly

Over the roofline little scuff
on the high brilliance. But moves

and not with the light breeze as seed
cluster or web might, but darts

and veers now into house shade, blue
needle, green darner in companionable zip

hither, over the gleaming car, back a bit, over
here, closer. Is this lake to be so

investigated, the car's shine
water-sheen? My polish, pheromone?

It's the way of animal to lead
the eye…   I too

have *follow, follow,* nothing else
in mind at times like ours

between, beyond the surfaces.
You knit, mend, the namers imagined.

Little comforter. Little blanket of attention
I'm snug under, watching wholly where

one goes anywhere in the air, precisely.
Or just there where the lengthy drooping point

of iris leaf, stirred in fervent half-circles
a moment in the breeze (that flippant

breeze I discounted) waves you down.

Toadal

I may as well sit on the big rock
island in seeded area, questing

as revisit our low squat
under swordfern beside
the broken clay pot, and

with heel of forelimb accomplish
the stuffing of foodstuffs into a corner
of horizontal smile, straight-faced

at the sideways flop. Ouch! Caustic
earth under the hot tub! Oh, jokes

aside, where

are you? I should take sharp shovel to rock
to spark from mud clod our medieval

being. Abiogenesis. A rougher, true
story of niche, grimace. No, go

bigger. Biopoiesis. We were then as
those come kilometres upslope

from marsh, mating. As those
sequestered in summer. Bidder's organs

still vestigial. You unlikely canary!

Sapsucker

This pair, these parents, have chosen
their tree, are head-banging narrow

rectangular windows open
in the bark. Their beaks

stroke the frames' edges upwards cupping (not
sucking) sap and the shaggy young flop about trying

the same, but mostly sloppily gulp from the parents.
In high summer later the leaves on the splendid

fountained array of branches brown and curl, but
"Hey," says Theresa, "you can't kill cotoneaster,"

and berries are forming, might brighten
to prove it, them, everything stubbornly

on its way in the world, that adolescent flinging
itself upon the screen door, clinging

and looking in, looking in. Us staring back
from the kitchen. A granular, sugary substance suddenly

encrusting the gap and the margins, already dusting
the shock… and this concoction/confection to come.

Lizard

Bask, you beauty, stretched
on the old sheathing, back limb negligently lapsed
tailwards, on the old plywood tarred

for its first roof role, its echoing rain-song, tar
patches flaking off now but you, beauty, negligent

of bare or toxic or sealed space basking there
on the modest ad hoc heights, new roof the plywood's

making over the old shakes stacked for kindling.
"You're a handsome fellow," I'm crooning

in greeting, my wife laughing into the phone
to our daughter, "Dad's just talking to his
best friend." "One," I'm allowing, "one

of my best friends." You beauty
on the used wood smiling

your alligator smile, last millimetre hook-
up of hairline lip-line at the jaw's crux.
Bluish beauty of the one eye my way, bask

as sun heightens, day brightens, shade
beckoning. Wife teases I've your skin
on my sun-damaged forearms

but that's a new tail you're sporting.
Bask, beauty, while we may.

Hair of the Dog

Outsized pup of my middle years I built
this overturned house for, the floor

torn apart for repair now all
there was when first she

nudged up onto it, claimed it
and had to be shoved off to let me get on

with the framing. Simple to turn and
turn, return (as any old dog does lying

down, settling in
to its box of habit and instinct)

with slick of stain again on my brush
in August, new nails for new shingle...

Simple to bestow almost insouciant
the killing clouds of Raid upon

carpenter ants in paroxysm restacking
their exposed pupae in a newly de-

constructed corner, open juncture revealing
a bristle in the joinery. Lily's, snagged

as she snuffled near the opening
it must have been. A little pinch...

Simple enough the rationale: *A matter*
of saving the structure, not getting a new

dog, or maybe. We'll see. In no time and
for weeks after looking in there's a delicate

complicated litter of termite wings the fall
winds don't stir much… all empty

dry interior invisibly at risk.

Cougar

This is the page where the animals mass
and cringe and scatter. Each from its singular

cage of cover, experience of encounter, breaks

out or scrabbles whimpering dog-like to get
under the plywood tent platform and you can stop

saying as so often some way into so many
present-day volumes of verse: *Someone*

had an idea. We got somehow from tent
to car, dog and me, out from under the scream

of the savaged baby (a certainty!)

in the rent June dawn where the lit house sits
and settles today, where no one in three decades

from any of its many windows, or bringing in
firewood, or strolling the acreage, has ever seen,

except for tracks some years back in snow, a cougar.

Kinship

No, this ark has sailed.
The great hulk listing

in its balm. On board two
by two via bible, board books

and these just in—by clump by smear by fission
(coral polyp, frog spawn, cloning protozoans)

from polar melts, your boggy yard, logged
Amazons—now disembarked… Dove circling,

circling… Apologies. Big enough beings
to lean to deep reflection, big enough to see

it's us, us first, us filtering, we've sucked it up
to grant splayed subjects of the cast-off kingdoms

language, tools, exotic powers—specious
niggardly benefits of our guilt. Beyond

that? Numbered, numberless
singularities, they sink towards

sunset to acidify, steam
or the metaphor rides out, rinses

to antithesis, to buoyant drift
of tar mat, data. Art too. *Oui*

c'est nous, le déluge—consciousness.
Expansive. Adaptive. Inclusive. Mass-

extinctive. Not big enough.

Bull

Museu Nacional de Arqueologia, Lisbon

Terracotta massif on a box on the polished
foyer floor: forelegs folded under, scars

of the tethers across the brow above
bulbous eyes pulled from the sides

of his head to our forward gape, blur...
Smiling? The signals are self-
conscious, sympathetic. An entrance...

His labours are not done.

Exhausted, imploring, he persists. We persist.
We pull. Twenty-seven centuries. The fields

not forgotten. The décor is sparse, conditioned.
Conditional nonetheless. Signage glosses

the wonder and the wound in *apotropaic pledge,
a password able to fend off the blows and ensure*

the Beatitudes. Going In to Collections
or Out to the pavements, the river, are big doors.

Codex Canadensis

Time to put the big book back
on the back shelf. Circled it

too long. It was the homey appeal
of the title, the charm of the drawings...

But opening with a tiger and a unicorn!
You will understand why from

the exegesis (*monstres*, things worth
showing) but poor poem! Cutting trail

again in strangeness, eccentricity
across the continent, the centuries

for one more shot at a sensible country? By rote
he went AWOL in the New World, Père Nicolas,

patron saint of a crazed correctness, building his book
back home in Old France, the authoritative models

to hand. Hence the "grey partridge" in fluffy muffler
to play a ruffed grouse. His beaver hunches and snarls,
an aquatic wolverine, but eschews (from Rondelet) the balls

displayed, the beast splayed overhead as if a flying frog
or fish. There's some fit to that staid category: fishy

and cagey as a spirit bear pacing an edge
of poster. O Canada! Oh fervent stiffness

with which the birds possess the pages
or tread another's head or back making room!
One with a red heart on its wing. Motifs
and complex hatching crowd every figure's
interior and the pipes of *les Indiens* flare
like volcanoes. These are dimensions

of lake glare, vertiginous forest
and secret strengths in the latitudes

seeming to put away the books, seeming to give ground
or defer outside the lines, the borders. These are founding
and confounding precedents, flat evidence, *a woman*

captured in war, whose nails were all pulled out
with teeth. I saw her burned in the village

of Toniotogéhaga for six (dix/ten?) hours...

And here is our elk, stub-legged and haggard
but insistently, *Elan ou caribou, alces*

selon les Latins... or a moose?

Gulls

Several on swells, sliding. The deep
is nothing to them, nor the vast air lifted

into. The snowy peaks, their empty
heads, the world before them. World

before us. None of it reflecting

upon peril as we do. Death there
transparent. Un-gulled by imaginings,

by apprehension. As it is everywhere
beyond us. As it is but in us. As it is.

Human

Here is its vaunted exceptionalism nude
a few steps from the house, bemused

by garter snake and lizard sunning
themselves in the ever-sought mossy

seam where hope and despair
share irrelevance despite the further

awareness taunting, thinking it knows
the real world is anachronism...

Not to mention clothing.
Not to mention language.

And there it goes shamed
and ingenuous shuffling back inside

its silly formulations of their greater
power (*I think I could turn*

and live with...) etc. with every
lesser gesture since towards

the species disappearing hourly
in its long-standing stupor standing.

Not to mention sadness.

Margined Burying Beetle

What are we each, exactly? Nothing
if not exacting
                        in response, articulate
in compensation… Succinct

in the tide of flesh-wrapped, flesh-
enraptured DNA at full, subsiding

in this bright world, dark world
of the solstice through which I am about

to carry the remainder
of my mother's remains

towards trees, these pond-sodden
roots she heeled in, crabapple

small and scabby of late but in the spring
a clustered mass of port wine glory above

wild iris. So I will go out next to her
hereafter, after my years rounded off today from

the day she bore me. So I will go out past her
going in any form or manner from this house

even as woodsmoke thinning out
in wind, or as a mouse under snow

nosing about—or as that one months back, long
flattened, desiccated on plush moss I (idly

pissing) spotted wondrously

shifting! The beetle beneath it is said to drag corpses
sixteen feet, is said to be nocturnal but nudged

the resurrection my way in sunlight, sinuous
wriggler chevroned orange on black, sinewy

writer of a future always
writhing on edge at the edges.

Insect Noise

You'd think the choruses: mosquito hum
at the screens or cicadas sounding out

a summer eve. But these were solos:
wing-rattling beetle above the car's

back shelf, nowhere discovered kilometres
later where we stopped; and just now the moth

that woke me shuddering against the bedroom's
western window, wanting out. You'd think it's about

sex, feeding, mystery, annoyance, a little
fear maybe. Not invisible

boundaries, dis-
location, last light.

THIS WAS THE RIVER

Near Greenwood

Arrow/Boundary Country

My grandfathers, my father, dead. Father-in-law
dying in Victoria, whose father worked here
circa 1911, in Phoenix, the townsite below

or rather the rubble remainder of townsite
mined through into open pit by '58. Our vista
from the relocated cenotaph, over graves...

I would have been eleven. Habitually these idle
chimes, correspondences, variances, paradoxes
to what end: lambs on the headstones of babes

and children? The pine
in wind on the mountain still.
On the way here from Osoyoos a shattered

deer on the maintenance truck's tailgate
at the viewpoint, again at the rest stop...
Really? That obvious? It's taking

these deaths, is it, all of them, to take us
off our beaten track through Midway
into backcountry, the dusty

grey-green mullein standing
at road edge, meadow edge, edge
of the tailing pond? Of course

we're getting closer. We are drawn.

"among the leaves so green o"

I know it was the darkest shading
in that we played on after sunset
by porch light, but did we divide

the heaps of clippings into portions, make
our fortunes, or bury each other, or pretend
to be farmers? Yes it was grass, a spring's

first thick mowing a decade or more
before I read Whitman's *beautiful uncut*
hair of graves and decades before I'm risking

this corruption of the wordless happiness.
Never closer, however it was we imagined
the world before being called in... Echoes

even then in the colour, in any mention
in myth and legend of green sward or green
wood... Robin Hood... Richard Greene

released the arrow that spun the titles *thunk*
and thrum into the tree first Saturday I stayed
awake late drinking cola, a caffeinated clarity

not blurred till boughs made bowers
unquiet for us, O lovely maids

in summer coming on... Drift of bright-
leafed aspen mist on the slopes beyond
the town in the distance.

Stack & Slag

A great part of huge earth
was scorched by the terrible vapour
and melted as tin melts when heated
by men's art in channelled crucibles…
— from "The War of the Titans," Hesiod

…so close their lithe and delicate greenery
to the stack, its quarter million bricks' worth

firm in the firmament a decommissioned
lifetime later, saplings edging

up to the slag heap, encroaching
upon the solidified mass, crowded

along the long draft tunnel's
collapsing parade route. Cheers!

On the travel blog the photographer's sons
shove and roughhouse under one

hell's bell, Titan's helmet, shape
of the slag pot's cooling shell

on the black slump battle-
field strewn with them. Molten

are our days, our earth, our high
thrust of the toxins skyward, time

the only Titan standing.

I Know

Mid-morning slash
of summer solstice sun honed
on roof ridges, aslant across the vacant

city lot, edges towards the doe
in the dirt heaving slightly, lifting
her head slightly towards her wet fawn's

nudges, sinking back. I mean right
downtown, right on Hwy 3. *I know,*

says the owner of the antiques shop
opposite, only place open, coming

out beneath his awning's shade to see.
I know. I'll call. But what can you do?

Copper Beech

No gods but what we want in passing.
Let's say this tree we're planting, leaf shine

behind the fine mesh
deer fence, marginal

protection. Ashes of parents
at root, eventual (centuries

hence) verdigris shade of canopy, *not
in our lives*
          in our thoughts, we

say looking that way.

No Hands

Cromeleque dos Almendres, Evora, Portugal

I was there but can't think now how
on the ground between them to be

among them, neolithic ovoids
of stone standing about, about

what? Presences void of our obsessions: sex,
death... and let's not guess gods or giants

scattering sand or their smatter of tears, active
as these are not doing (arms) going (legs) limbs

bound as yet within the bodies—or pre-bodies, un-
differentiated eggs? Expertise first figured

each figure a phallus, then clan, family—or fancy makes
listeners of several leaning towards another. But only one

of more than ninety is rendered as we are
best pleased to see each other: individual, distinct,

a person.   Or heresy assembled

from older icons on the other stones: shepherd's crook
cross-slant to ground from slant of the upright boulder's

shoulder, crescent moon cupped a little higher, circles
above blunt wedge now nose, tricky pixellation

in the pitted granite zoomed into close-up
as fingers today might spread, expand a screen

for the face. To see the face, source and pivot
of eons-long triangulations to exactly place

this fan-shaped eastward-tipping slope where
all the dawns comply *menir*

to *menir*, solstice to solstice—to
eyeball! Each companionable height, each

warming stone stroked down with sunlight, measure. Seers
all, all at once reset on a chiselled cusp in the fourth or fifth
millennium BCE... notion then as now at play, leap-

frogging means, meaning. Personage
from what's to hand. From nowhere
a crowd. No hands. First graffiti.

High Regard

Kelly Samra Pass, b. July 17, 2014

Along your street newborn
in the sheltering elms, winged
seed greening, fame—

a million iterations
of the heart of your name.

Beringian

What from the evidence? From the fossil
record, the great beasts still unfolding

from the hills, from the pollen
and DNA, from millennial

traceries of ice sheets, ocean
levels, from the deep-

water drilling, what? What
from the sediments, the litter of old

settlements? A figure alone at the shore (familiar

smudge of awe and purpose in the mist) hunched
seaward past rocky outcrop, drift logs, tide line:

the east or the south or the west in his eyes. So much
as that. This much at least on the bridge called

home: ridges of glacier, climax forest or flowering
tundra at our backs, wide swaths of steppe

or freeway into the continents. Rough terrain
of language edging everything in and out

of understanding. Biome shift. Some nights, neon
waves of particles from the north. But lost

daylight lifting us daily. Sea glass or
spear point or cellphone lifted to it.

Holding Arthur

Arthur Émile Labelle Pass, b. October 7, 2015

Holding Arthur (fifteen days old) the day after
seeing the Pompeii exhibit, holding him

by the window, blurred and ashen birds
settling in the maples' umber. Holding Arthur's

unfocused reaching. Holding his sleep-
ing breathing, as if holding the rest

of the world, the day
after Pompeii.

Unreasonable Facsimile Thereof

In old ways you might sing
the jingle or speak

the phrase that pays
or scrawl a logo for the contest—
idly or in homeless hope might print upon

a scrap of paper SHELL
or DUZ. Submission, submission
does the work. Like this—

legible, eligible, fastidious, as if
from outside a self awaiting
your taking note

awaiting your inhabitation, new
ways in. As if you might win
what you are.

Look

Henry Byron Pass, b. September 7, 2016

In the hubbub of celebration, everyone
looking and talking at you, your look (we

cannot say seeing) at and through
and past us is it, over our shoulders?

Startled, a little bit skeptical, knowing beyond
your few walleyed hours (what?

you cannot say). We looking your way not
where you see, talking and talking, saying

what we will.

Poetry Month

Under urgent skies in the sharp sunshine
of prizes to be, or *shoures soote*, I'm out

scrubbing and scraping moss and mould
off the old flat surfaces, the decks

and patio. Ache and effort
and slippery recollection and

tulips at the edge. And how many years
of this left to me? Intermittent

satisfactions with the hose, green
swill. Finalist? Check

the website every couple
of hours. Win or no

is the same prognosis. Days go, leafing
traceries. Keep at bud and grime.

Pleasure Craft

Weeks after I want to know
what I'm holding onto, how

the languorous hold (ambivalent,
needy) of that evening upon me

was accomplished on the pretty
surfaces, the intricate harbour busy

in every cove and corner with summer traffic,
the business of fun on the water. There goes

a Sea-Doo, a young couple clutching atop it, him waving...
disappearing thread of bikini bottom flagging her straddling

ass a last glimpse in passing. Here is an antique schooner
beautifully restored, and here a giant cruiser sporting

military radar laced to a little rowboat pier.
It was the grand tour my friends, our ninety-minute

chug-about after the chamber music in the changed
landscape, the waterfront landmarks (a half-hour apart

by road) shoulder to shoulder from our afloat perspective leaning
in or out a bit the way friends do in conversation or arranging

themselves to be photographed. But for the complication
of the ladder I would have swum at some point before

we returned to the dock so close to the tarred pilings
and stilled propellers. The steaks were delicious. Who imagined

a plate-sized aluminum barbeque you could clamp to a deck rail?
In this cul-de-sac off the whale-road how is it each hull

is a perfect fit into water but a poem's fit to fullness flubs it?
Only the clumsy synaptic scoop/slur of language? Wayward

wavelets? An oily light is shifting, shimmies. What is its quarrel
with contentment? My queasy angst only of surfeit, aging?

In this trampled paddock of the trackless sea where landfall
lolls in every direction, where home is to hand in numinous

crannies of clever invention, with our asses covered in every
(airy) dimension and the stars emerging as superfluous

to navigation as the sleeping standby computer pilot,
we generators hum the idling, tireless sum of our skill.

Blue Blazers

Days like these in cloudless July
a neighbour calls *blue blazers.*

Through low, wide-open, south-
facing windows pungent massed

tangle of tomato plants, lilies
towering at the stair rail, a flaring

reprise of roses, stupefied
trees... Here's to a list as long

as my life takes its crest its rest it can make
no ending. Listless, confounded, semi-

formal, a body slurs on
at the speed of plants, hauled

upright by its collar-cum-corolla
for a carbon encore, dusted

down, re-dressed in flame, hazy
echoes of mumbles, *We've got this*

(we're Management, wait staff, first responders).
Coming through here... with the stretchers, flow-

charts, trays of lemonade? *Coming through*
vista, eon, the pith of the shade.

Results

These are the results to be hoped for, those
you most wanted yesterday that say

with the specialist's flourish turning
over the printout, *Here's what we*

determine: notwithstanding false
negatives, your life's duration is undetermined

again. Refold the opened
envelope to overhear your musings

to a friend tomorrow or next
year, *Well, I could be hit by a bus, but...*

But don't you miss just a little the nagging
frisson of alertness in every thought

that brought into focus a smudge
of grief in bright leaf and idiot pity for

passersby, the surprising resistance
you found in yourself

to pointless panic and regret... Don't you
miss just a little the intimate beckoning certainty?

Purples

Pansies sporting their tattered purples
against the concrete retaining wall

at the foot of the stairs to the pool.
Brittle, leggy, browner, bedded

annuals between. It's November.
Struggle is all. Or to everything

a season. Choose your closure.
Yet there is none. Open amidst

clenched hope, sadness, fear—
here are friends, conviviality!

Under the steepening lean of loss, talk
and laughter. Bright, bruised pennants.

Harrowing

For months he'd believed she
was doomed, would suffer, and suffer
treatment, and die. And he'd live on, inconsolable.

The firs were darker than winter sky, already
lost property, everything loved become nothing
without her. Their beloved place on earth, nowhere.

But a campsite with friends as quickly attained
as ascertained: that one across the turbulent creek,
white dinghy flipped and aswirl in the muddy eddy!
Get the car out there over the logs lashed together and

we'll have it to ourselves. And the hummocky shore horizon
across the Flemish floodplain from the promontory. A swim
before dinner beside the male ibex skittish in surf/mist?

Too cold yet (don't push the season) and too far reading
the rock at one's feet, an I-spline in relief abutting
vague iconography sketching in *suspended*

*touch between individuals of the same
species—all there is.* No block of lines laying out
vines' hold, buds' hope. No stanza. One word, one

gleaming disc in turned sod, opened meaty furrow.

Little Ropes

Where to lob the little ropes
of hope? Was that a post, the pier?
I second-guess and second-guess

as my fears for her, for me, crest
and trough, extrapolate. In the squall

all loops and snarl, gnarled fistful this
of knotted throwing end: we live.

Solely the Embrace Endures

Brno-Malomerice jug, National Museum, Prague

Solely the embrace endures but that (however
long the stretch) a bronze encompassing

default, default of firmer substance yet
than the wooden gourd decayed

to disappearance through its fingers: fine
openwork retains the form but shapelessness

flows also in the loose air all directions
through the casting... *So be it*, one

might say, anachronistic turn of phrase
against the emptied, agèd gleam appropriate

enough: wan sentiment and tiresome
tug (that hugging, or its artifact, lives on)

dispensed with thus... So such a one as you or I
swum in and floating (cheek and ear and temple

pressed upon the lakeshore's sun-warmed
rock) concurs, or at the very least

knows not. He's come (how simply!) as far before
(to ground) and has no hint (nor hankering) this

instant re further. A default
of water holds him...

                                            as water holds
the tree frog tadpole in the terracotta pot—

lip at the seam of glaze and air and liquid
light suspended, creature that may yet ascend

to emerald on sticky digits, to rose
leaf and stair rail, to have its digital portrait done

perchance beside the little-finger nail
of the swimmer's hand, for contrast. *Limit*

to the limitless plead measure/metaphor
but their screen and net (*unlikeliness/un-*

likeness meshed) assay the ant
I flicked from your damp towel

towards the lake. Out beyond its furthest chance
past thoughtlessness (and thinking) (as zooms up

a breadth of sheen, a surface to support
more thrashing) wells there, well yes, a

depth to bear
the sinking after.

Tug

Edmond Richard Labelle Pass, b. July 3, 2018

As the news came, minute by minute, hour
by hour, in excited phone calls, digital photos

of you on the scales, in your parents'
arms, at the Korean restaurant...

I was building a little deck. I was pulling garlic.
I wish you all the wonders of our skills—

quickness, structure, flavour, vistas... but

moreso this—the deeply whole, forgiving tug
of good things from the ground.

Jim Harrison

Jim Harrison's last book came out
early in the year he died, 2016, an up-

and-down time for everyone. He numbers
stuff a lot in the poems. Like birds: millions, a

thousand, five thousand, two… and his age, as old
people always do with some confounded

wonder. Even the dust jacket mentions
his seventies. I just turned that page myself

and sent dear friends a poem to tell them.
Anik, in Amsterdam, sent me Jim's book

published in Port Townsend, three
short ferry rides down the coast from here.

He's a shaggy, smoking gnome on the cover.
Spirited off and all over with Machado,

Mandelstam, Rumi, Lorca, he's brought
the whole gang home, or near enough

to hear him chortling out there, leaned
back under the snow. My favourite line

at first was in "Bird Nightmares": *people
were reduced to reading poetry because*

it was shorter. But best at last is the last
line of the last poem after his very last

frequent (but singular, numberless) pretty girl...
tracking the edge of the universe from his bridge-

work ending into it: *the sky, the sea, the faint
green streak of Canadian forest on the far shore.*

This Was the River

This was the river hiked dreaming upstream
dropping gear and then clothing for the full

brown pull of surrendered connection, deliverance.
Starting downhill in Lillooet, the picnic table

puddled with yesterday's socked-in drizzle (dark
we drove up in) retweets in patches an opening

gleam in the sky onto sandbar, bench-lands.
From muddled movement, mud,

to step unexpectedly into refreshment, swirled
palette of eddy-boil, gravels and boulders, sure-

footed map of the island adjacent picked
up in a seed potato of pebble! Pine

root and cacti are hugging the clay banks
and sluices. Bunchgrass. Bird's nest

in a small tree's last gold
leaves. Scenes past season in new amber.

Contentment. Tormented a year since
it cannot be our hurt earth holds

consolation (limitless!) out to us
still. But is. Naive to believe it. But is

(old guess) my sole way forward, suspension
bridge under repair just over there.

Watching Surfers at Cox Bay

The edge of a wildness pulls them out, wild
in their bodies as it was in a world bigger

than our mess of it. Almost infinite
it seemed again on the long road in

or in idly pondering how many waves
to Japan. Past nuclear waste and too

much CO_2, out beyond the space junk
is our edge now. Over the Great Pacific

Garbage Patch. Fixedly they chase the swells
for the rhythm of return, the *at-one-with*

our oldest pulse. Girl in the coffee house making
earrings names every beach from Malibu north.

Soft eyes, fresh skin. Mist past the point in
a listening sky as I take off my glasses.

Notes on the Poems

"Rereading My Notes re Rereading *Clea* in Venice": *Clea*, Lawrence Durrell, Faber and Faber, London, 1960.

"Open Question": The Wendell Berry quote is from "Look It Over" in *Leavings*, Counterpoint, Berkeley, 2010.

"A Cheering Stain": "like a piece of ice on a hot stove the poem must ride on its own melting," Robert Frost, from his essay "The Figure a Poem Makes."

"New Town Hall": Construction of Prague's New Town Hall started shortly after the founding of New Town by Charles IV in 1348.

"Creation of the Animals": Tintoretto, oil on canvas c. 1551, Gallerie dell'Accademia, Venice.

"Dragonfly": "blue needle" and "green darner" are common dragonfly names.

"Toadal": Abiogenesis is the origin of life or living organisms from inorganic or inanimate substances; historically, spontaneous generation. Biopoiesis is a process by which living organisms are thought to develop from nonliving matter, and the basis of a theory on the origin of life on Earth. The Bidder's organ is found in most members of the family Bufonidae (true toads).

"Lizard": northern alligator lizard, *Elgaria caerulea*.

"Kinship": *Oui c'est nous, le déluge* chimes off *Après nous, le déluge*—Madame de Pompadour, 1757.

"Codex Canadensis": *The Codex Canadensis and the Writings of Louis Nicolas*, François-Marc Gagnon ed., with Nancy Senior and Réal Ouellet, McGill-Queens University Press, Montreal, 2011.

"Human": "I think I could turn and live with animals…" Walt Whitman, "Song of Myself."

"Margined Burying Beetle": *Nicrophorus marginatus* buries dead mice for the incubation of its eggs and the feeding of its larvae.

"Arrow/Boundary Country": a region of south central British Columbia. Phoenix was a copper-mining town near Greenwood BC, where the ore was smelted.

"Copper Beech": *Fagus sylvatica*. The Old English *bōc* and Old Norse *bók* both have the primary sense of "beech" but also a secondary sense of "book," and it is from *bōc* that the modern word derives.

"High Regard": The name Samra is a variant of samara, the winged seed of elms and maples.

"Beringian": Recent archaeological discoveries of settlements offshore on the northwestern coast of North America suggest that Beringians may have migrated down the coast while adjacent inland areas remained icebound and inaccessible.

"Poetry Month": "Whan that Aprill with his shoures soote", is the opening line of the Prologue to *The Canterbury Tales*, Geoffrey Chaucer, circa 1390.

"Solely the Embrace Endures": All that remains today of the Brno-Malomerice jug is the bronze lattice work that enwrapped the original wooden vessel.

"Watching Surfers at Cox Bay": "Mist past the point in…" The northwesterly tip of Cox Bay near Tofino, BC, is Pettinger Point.

Acknowledgements

Thanks to the editors of *Arc, Cascadia Magazine, Grain, Prairie Fire, The Malahat Review, The New Quarterly, Terrain.org, Vallum* and *Watershed Sentinel* where some of these poems first appeared.

"A Cheering Stain" was a finalist in the 2017 *Terrain.org* Poetry Contest (*Terrain: A Journal of the Built + Natural Environments*).

The book's central sequence, Creation of the Animals, is for Angelica Pass. An earlier version of the poem sequence was a finalist for the *Malahat Review* Long Poem Prize in 2015.

"Margined Burying Beetle" won the *Malahat Review* Open Season Award in 2016.

"Deer" appeared in *Prairie Fire* and was subsequently chosen for inclusion in *The Best Canadian Poetry in English, 2018* (Tightrope Books).

The Frank O'Hara quote is from "Heroic Sculpture" in *Selected Poems*, Vintage, New York, 1974.

"Copper Beech" was printed by the poet at High Ground as a keepsake in celebration of his seventieth birthday, December 2017.

"Holding Arthur" and "Tug" and earlier versions of "High Regard" and "Look" were printed by the poet at High Ground as keepsakes in celebration of the births of his grandchildren.

"Pleasure Craft" is for Robin and Jillian Ridington.

"Purples" is for Andrew Scott and Katherine Johnston.

"Jim Harrison" is for Anik See. Lines quoted are from "Bird Nightmares" and "Bridge" in *Dead Man's Float*, Copper Canyon Press, Port Townsend, 2016.